Biographies of famous people to support
the National Curriculum.

# Elizabeth I

## by Harriet Castor
## Illustrations by Peter Kent

**W**

FRANKLIN WATTS

LONDON • NEW YORK • SYDNEY

First published in 1996 by
Franklin Watts
96 Leonard Street
London
EC2A 4RH

Franklin Watts Australia
14 Mars Road
Lane Cove
NSW 2066

© 1996 text Harriet Castor
© 1996 illustrations Peter Kent
This edition 1998
The right of the author to be identified
as the author of this work, has been asserted.

The right of the illustrator to be identified
as the illustrator of this work, has been asserted.

ISBN: 0 7496 2415 9

A CIP catalogue record for this book
is available from the British Library.

Dewey Decimal Classification Number: 942.05

10 9 8 7 6 5 4 3

Series editor: Sarah Ridley
Designer: Kirstie Billingham
Consultants: David Wray and Dr Anne Millard

Printed in Great Britain

# Elizabeth I

In 1533, a royal baby was born.
The father was Henry VIII,
King of England, and the
mother was Anne Boleyn, the
second of his six wives.

They called the baby Elizabeth.

King Henry was disappointed.
He and his first wife had
already had one daughter,
Mary, and now he wanted a son.

He thought only boys were
any good at ruling countries.

Henry didn't know what
a great and famous queen
Elizabeth would turn out to be.

Later Henry and his third wife did have a son, called Edward.

Edward and Elizabeth got on well. They both studied hard and wrote each other letters in Latin!

When Henry died, Edward
became king, even though
he was only nine.

But he didn't live long.

Next, Elizabeth's older sister –
Mary Tudor – became queen.

At this time, people argued a lot
about the right way to worship
God. One group were called
Protestants. The other group
were called Catholics.

King Edward had said everyone
should be Protestant. Now Mary
Tudor said everyone should be
Catholic. No wonder there were
lots of arguments!

Mary even made Elizabeth a prisoner in the Tower of London for following the wrong religion. Mary was afraid people might try to push her off the throne and put Elizabeth there instead.

Watch it, Bob – she could be queen one day!

Elizabeth was very brave, even though she was in danger of having her head chopped off.

When Elizabeth was 25, Mary died. Now, at last, Elizabeth was queen!

The first thing everyone said she should do was to get married, because people still thought women weren't good at ruling countries. They wanted her to have children, too.

But Elizabeth didn't want to
marry. She didn't want a
husband telling her what to do.

Elizabeth was ruler of England, Wales and parts of Ireland.

Scotland had its own queen, Mary Queen of Scots. Mary and Elizabeth never met, but Elizabeth asked other people what Mary looked like. She was jealous in case Mary was more beautiful than her.

Elizabeth loved dancing and
music. She wrote some poetry
too, and was famous for being
an excellent horse-rider.

But Elizabeth wasn't the sort of ruler who just had fun all day and left the governing of the country to others. She worked very hard. Often, she was at work with her ministers before dawn.

And Elizabeth wasn't always easy to work with. Though she was often cheerful and witty, she also had a terrible temper.

She once threw her slipper at
one of her ministers, and spat
at a courtier she was cross with.
Her maids of honour often
got slapped.

In public, though, Elizabeth was gracious and kind. She wanted the ordinary people to love her and be loyal to her.

She wanted to impress them,
too. So, for public appearances,
she always put on her most
magnificent clothes.

One of her dresses was decorated
with a thousand seed pearls.

Though Elizabeth had expensive clothes, she was still very careful with money. If even the smallest jewel fell off a dress or cloak and was lost, she had it carefully noted down.

Anyone found the diamond yet?

I thought she just wanted us to kneel!

Sometimes she even sold off
some of her personal possessions
to get a bit of extra cash.

One of the most expensive
things a ruler could do was go
to war. So Elizabeth wanted
to avoid it.

But in 1588 she didn't have
a choice.

The trouble was, Elizabeth was
a Protestant, and some Catholic
rulers of other countries wanted
to push her off the throne and
put a Catholic there instead.

One candidate was Mary Queen of Scots. Mary had been pushed off her own throne by the Scottish Protestants and had fled to England.

The Queen of Scots is a danger to me. Lock her up!

Even under lock and key, Mary kept plotting to have Elizabeth killed so she could seize her throne.

Eventually, after 19 years, and yet another plot, Elizabeth ordered Mary's head to be chopped off.

But that wasn't the end of the
danger. The Catholic King
of Spain, Philip, wanted to
make England a Catholic
country again.

So, in 1588, Philip decided
to invade. He sent a fleet of
ships, called the Armada, to
attack England.

Elizabeth's spies told her the Armada was coming, so she got her own ships ready.

Elizabeth's ships were much smaller than Philip's. But the English sailors had a clever idea.

They loaded some empty ships with gunpowder and set them on fire. Then they pushed them towards the Armada.

Luckily, the wind carried on blowing the 'fire-ships' the right way!

The Spaniards were terrified
when they saw the fire-ships.
They tried to sail away as fast
as possible, but their ships were
so big and clumsy that some
bumped into each other!

The English ships chased them.
Then there was a terrible storm
and most of the great Spanish
ships sank.

Meanwhile, back on shore,
hundreds of soldiers were getting
ready to fight the Spaniards if
they landed.

Elizabeth went to see them.
She told the soldiers that, just
because she was a woman, it
didn't mean she was scared –
she was as brave as any king.

When the news finally came
that the Armada was beaten,
everyone was very relieved.

Poems were written in
celebration, and there was

a magnificent procession to
St Paul's Cathedral for a
thanksgiving service. Elizabeth
rode in a chariot with a golden
canopy, pulled by white horses.

Elizabeth didn't only go out amongst her people when there was a crisis or a special celebration.

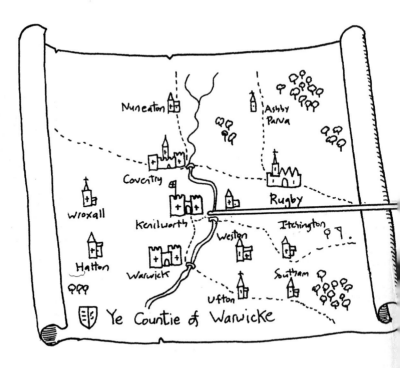

Ye Countie of Warwicke

In peacetime, to let as many of her subjects as possible see her, Elizabeth went on 'progresses'. She and her courtiers travelled about the country, staying with important people on the way.

Travelling was very slow and difficult. They could only go about three miles an hour, and no more than twelve miles a day. If the weather was bad it was even slower.

No wonder Elizabeth called the journey from London to Bristol "long and dangerous"!

Having Elizabeth to stay
was a great honour. But it
was also dreadfully expensive.
It wasn't just the food; gifts
and special entertainments
were expected, too.

One host had a big lake dug
in his garden, with man-made
islands in it, for a play. And
Elizabeth was only staying for
three days!

When Elizabeth finally died,
aged 69, she had been queen for
nearly 45 years. Because she
had no children, the crown
passed to the son of Mary Queen

of Scots: King James VI of
Scotland. He became King
James VI and I, and ever since
then, the countries of the
'United Kingdom' have shared
the same monarch.

# Further facts

## Tudor Toiletries

Elizabeth was famed for being very clean.

People were amazed that she had a bath once every three months – whether she needed it or not!

Although Elizabeth's teeth went black in old age, it wasn't because she didn't clean them. She rubbed them with a cloth and used toothpicks too.

The water-closet (WC) was invented by a godson of Elizabeth, John

Harington. Elizabeth was so impressed with his idea that she had one installed at her palace at Richmond.

Her court, though, carried on using loos that didn't flush. They were cleaned out only when the court moved on to a different palace. *Then* somebody had a very smelly job!

### Fresh Talent

In Elizabeth's reign, there was a new actor and playwright in London called William Shakespeare. Some of his plays – which are some of the most famous plays ever written – were performed before Elizabeth herself.

# Some Important Dates
# in Elizabeth I's Lifetime

**1533**   Elizabeth is born, the second daughter of Henry VIII.

**1536**   Elizabeth's mother, Anne Boleyn, is ordered to be executed by her husband, Henry VIII.

**1547**   Henry VIII, Elizabeth's father, dies. Her brother, Edward, becomes king.

**1553**   Edward VI dies and Elizabeth's older sister, Mary, is crowned queen.

**1554**   Elizabeth is imprisoned in the Tower of London by Mary I.

**1558**   Mary I dies and Elizabeth is crowned queen.

**1587**   After many years of plots and intrigues by Mary Queen of Scots, Elizabeth orders her execution.

**1588**   Philip of Spain sends a fleet of Spanish ships, called the Armada, to invade England. The English fleet wins and the danger passes.

**1603**   Elizabeth dies at the age of 69 years old.